SCARS OF ALMOST

beautiful then broken

NIHARIKA MOTYANI

Copyright © <2025> <Niharika Motyani>

All Rights Reserved.

This book has been self-published with all reasonable efforts taken to make the material error-free by the author. No part of this book shall be used, reproduced in any manner whatsoever without written permission from the author, except in the case of brief quotations embodied in critical articles and reviews.

The Author of this book is solely responsible and liable for its content including but not limited to the views, representations, descriptions, statements, information, opinions and references ["Content"]. The Content of this book shall not constitute or be construed or deemed to reflect the opinion or expression of the Publisher or Editor. Neither the Publisher nor Editor endorse or approve the Content of this book or guarantee the reliability, accuracy or completeness of the Content published herein and do not make any representations or warranties of any kind, express or implied, including but not limited to the implied warranties of merchantability, fitness for a particular purpose. The Publisher and Editor shall not be liable whatsoever for any errors, omissions, whether such errors or omissions result from negligence, accident, or any other cause or claims for loss or damages of any kind, including without limitation, indirect or consequential loss or damage arising out of use, inability to use, or about the reliability, accuracy or sufficiency of the information contained in this book.

Made with ❤ on the Notion Press Platform

www.notionpress.com

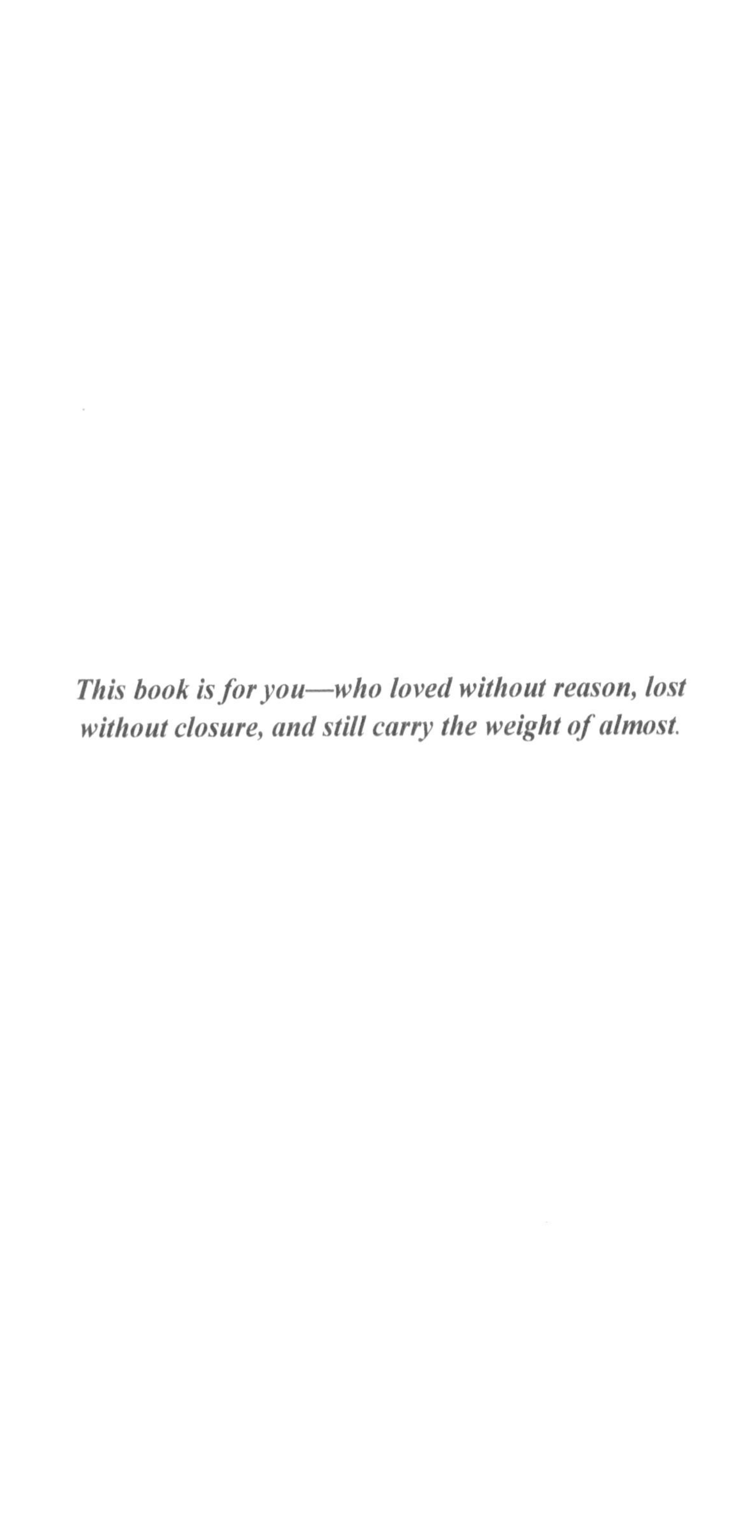

This book is for you—who loved without reason, lost without closure, and still carry the weight of almost.

This book is not just a collection of poems—it is journey through the quiet ache of unspoken love, the weight of almosts, and the echoes of emotions left unsaid. Every page holds a piece of a heart that once hoped, broke, and learned to carry its scars with grace.

You may find yourself in these words, in the longing, the nostalgia, or the bittersweet beauty of what could have been. Let this book be a companion to your own feelings, a reminder that even the pain of almost-love is still a love worth remembering

Dear reader, I love you.

There will come a time when you must make peace with
the fact that those who were supposed to love you
couldn't do it in the way you needed—or maybe they
never could at all.

You will have to accept this without trying to undo it,
without wishing it were different. Instead, let it go and
turn inward.

Learn to give yourself the love they couldn't.

When I first looked at you, I swore I saw forever,

A spark, a whisper, a promise in disguise.

I never thought *you'd* be the one to leave me

Counting scars instead of stars in my eyes.

Now, when I look at you, I don't see magic,

I see every time I swallowed my pride,

Every hope I held like fragile glass,

Every moment *I wished* to be by your side.

I see you in dreams, where you don't belong,

A ghost in the night, a whisper, a song.

No day has passed without you in mind,

A cruel little curse, a love left behind.

You were my best friend, my shelter, my light,

Now just a shadow that haunts me at night.

I don't even want you—God knows that's true,

But the scars you left still burn like new.

Why does losing you feel like a knife in my chest?

A wound that won't heal, a pain that won't rest.

Why does letting you go tear me apart?

Like ripping my soul straight out of my heart.

I gave you my all, every piece, every part,

Thought you were the sun,

but you swallowed the dark.

You weren't the best thing—I see that now,

You shattered me, yet I still ask how.

I hate what you did, the ruin, the pain,

But somehow, I get it—I make no claims.

You never deserved me, not even a bit,

Yet some nights I miss you, I'll never admit.

A love undeserved, a bond now decayed,

Yet echoes of you refuse to fade.

I carry the weight, I bear the cost,

Of loving someone who left me lost.

I carry you within me, quietly,

like the ocean carries salt.

always there, unseen.

I carry you like the trees bear their branches,

like the night holds tight to the moon.

I search for you in everyone I meet,

resent them all, for none are you.

I won't let another soul close

none can touch me like you do

And the saddest truth lies clear

you don't fit my world, nor I yours,

yet every inch of me aches for you.

To stand before you, forced to look away—

every nerve in my body betrays me,

 my eyes forever lost, searching for you.

We never spoke the words, but we knew—
you never said you loved me; I never told you too.
And yet it was all we felt, all we needed.
every night since you've gone, I wonder

was anything real? Or was I just a shadow
you passed through, nothing more than a moment?
I broke myself to make space for you,
and maybe, someday, this ache will end
and leave something worth holding onto.

Something in you drags me near,

A pull so fierce, yet soaked in fear.

I meet the world, but all feels wrong—

They're not you, where I belong.

What's wrong with me? I cannot tell,

This endless ache, a private hell.

We break apart, but find our way,

A force unseen won't let us stray.

Is it my weakness that I stay?

A fool who can't let go your name?

Or do you feel this pain, this fire,

This endless loop of raw desire?

I crave to be the place you run,

When life feels lost, when battles won.

I want your storms, your cracks, your scars,

The fragile parts that make you ours.

So many years, and still, you haunt my mind,

Through every loss, I try to find

A piece of you in someone new,

But every road leads back to you.

I want your chaos, all your flaws,

Your quiet pain, your unhealed cause.

Though we are nothing, still it seems,

We're tied together in shattered dreams.

This love is cruel, it burns, it stings,

It tears apart, yet mends the strings.

I bleed for you, this endless fight,

Praying it leads us toward the light.

And even if this pain won't fade,

I'd hold it all—the mess we made.

For though we have nothing, we have it all,

And in your shadow, I still fall.

Niharika Motyani

I'm so dumb—

I know what you want from me.

It's written in the way your hands roam,

Not in the way they stay.

I see it clearly when you touch me—

It's not love.

The heat of your breath whispers lies,

A promise never meant to be kept.

You crave my body, not my soul,

The urge to destroy me,

But never to hold me.

You wreck my insides,

Between my legs,

Between my ribs,

Where my heart used to be whole.

You take from me,

But never take me.

You should be kissing my thoughts,

But you only devour my skin.

Your hands worship my body,

But never my being.

And still, I stay—

Because when your lips graze my neck,

When your hands claim what was once mine,

For just a moment,

I can pretend this is love.

I know it isn't.

But God, why do you make me feel like it is?

What have I become?

Hollow and numb,

A shadow of myself,

Lost in the love I gave you,

Fading while you thrived.

I bled to meet your needs,

Yet your actions carve wounds deep.

You make me scream in silence,

Tear my soul while I wear calm.

Why can't I let you go?

Why do you let go of me,

Only to return,

To twist the blade again?

Is it fun to toy with me,

To weave care into cruelty?

You make me believe,

Then you break me anew.

Each forgiveness chips away at me,

Leaving me smaller, weaker,

Still yearning for you.

Why can't I let you go?

What are you?

What am I?

Just a ghost in this endless ache,

A prisoner of your fleeting love.

Why do we circle back to this pain?

If we're not meant to be, why call my name?

You don't want me, yet you appear—

Only to leave me drowning in fear.

Why do you hurt me, then disappear?

Each time you're near, I shed a tear.

Reaching for you feels like a fight,

A pathetic plea in the dead of night.

Where is the man I once adored?

Now you're cruel, your words a sword.

You make me sick, you make me ache,

This love is a dream I can't unmake.

Our mornings were joy, our nights were bliss,

How did we end up lost like this?

Your laugh, your warmth, the way we'd share—

A broken heart still lingers there.

I don't want you back; it's not your face,

I miss the comfort, the fleeting grace.

But now, anxiety fills the air,

And panic whispers, "He's not there."

Niharika Motyani

It's been years, but time lies to me—

The clock ticks, but my heart stays still.

years since I touched your hair,

Since your hands played in mine,

Since your laughter painted my skies.

Was it truly years ago

That I last held you close,

Felt the weight of your arms,

Hugged you like I'd never let go?

How cruel, this distance, this empty air.

I still miss you, you know.

Not just the love we let slip through,

But you, my best friend, my anchor—

The piece of me I lost when I lost you.

I've been hollow ever since.

46

What went wrong?

Where did we falter, where did we break?

I replay the moments, the words unsaid,

Hoping to find the crack in our fragile bond.

But it always comes back to this—

An ache that never fades.

It's been years, but I'm frozen in time,

Still reaching for a shadow, a ghost.

I miss you, I miss us, I miss who I was.

Tell me, do you miss me too? Or am I alone,

Holding on to a memory you've let go?

You look at me like you feel something,

Touch me like you love me, soft and longing.

When the world gets heavy and shadows fall,

I'm the one you run to, I answer it all.

Am I just a toy you like to hold?

A fleeting warmth when the world turns cold?

If you don't feel, why do you pretend?

Why let me believe this will never end?

Am I dumb to think you'd care?

To keep calling, hoping you'd be there?

Your voice, I thought, would bring me calm,

But you only leave my heart in harm.

You make me feel incapable, weak,

Though I'd give my all, the love you seek.

Yet here I stand, a fool for you,

Bleeding for love that was never true.

I burn for you, a fire untamed,

Each flicker whispers your name.

I bleed for you, my veins run dry,

Yet you stand still, watching me cry.

52

I ache for you, a hollow refrain,

Each heartbeat screams your name in vain.

Your presence heals, your absence stings,

A cruel, unyielding pendulum swings.

I want you—every inch, every scar,

But you remain a distant star.

Your touch, your words, they pull me near,

Yet your silence ignites my deepest fear.

I dream of giving what you deserve,

But I spiral down a fragile curve.

To cook, to care, to hear your voice,

In your chaos, I would rejoice.

But what is this? What have I become?

A shadow chasing a fleeting sun.

I'm killing my pride, I'm losing my way,

For moments that break me every day.

Your actions scream what your lips won't say,

A bitter truth I can't replay.

Do you feel it too, or is it just me,

Drowning in love that will never be?

Who gives this much, who aches this deep?

I cry for you, I lose my sleep.

Perhaps it's love, or perhaps it's pain,

An endless storm with no refrain.

I burn, I bleed, I ache, I cry—

For a love that's mine to deny.

But still, I stay, despite the cost,

Loving you, knowing I'm lost.

Do you hear my crying,

Or did you choose to drown me out?

Is my pain too loud for you,

Or is silence what you're about?

I whisper your name in the wind,

But it never reaches your ear.

You walk through my storm untouched,

While I drown in what you don't hear.

Did you press mute on my sorrow,

Turn the volume of us down low?

Or was I always just background noise,

A song you never meant to know?

In my dreams, I make you pasta,

Soft and warm, like we used to be.

You sit, you smile, nothing is broken,

Nothing bad has happened to us.

The water bubbles, the sauce is thick,

I hum a song you once loved.

You reach for me, and I don't flinch—

Here, we are still whole.

But morning comes, the kitchen is quiet,

No scent of garlic, no sound of you.

Just an empty plate, a colder world,

And a love that only lives in dreams

My head betrayed me last night

With a dream of you and me—

Our hands still reaching,

Our voices still soft.

I woke with the taste of you in my breath,

The weight of your name in my chest,

And look—

How we bleed from all this wanting.

64

I killed a plant once

Because I gave it too much water.

Lord, I worry

That love is violence.

I wanted to give you everything—

Held you too close,

Spoke too sweetly,

Loved too much.

And now, look.

You wilted in my arms.

There comes a point, I told myself,

At which something is,

For better or for worse, finished.

Yes, I told you.

Of course, I had considered this possibility.

Accepting it would be something else.

Still, still, still.

Even in endings, I find you.

You were a great and terrible thing, to have loved.

Parts of me still remind me of you—

A certain laugh, a certain sigh.

I loved you to the point of ruin.

I loved you until my lungs were filled with ash.

And yet, the embers glow,

And yet, the love is there.

Still, still, still

Loving you was the last thing

I was really good at.

68

There are all kinds of love in the world,

But never the same love twice.

I held onto ours like a promise,

Like a prayer unspoken.

But tell me,

Was it ever truly mine to keep?

And is this not treason?

My soul belongs far more to you

Than it does to me.

To love you was to abandon myself.

To lose you was to become hollow.

I want everything back, the way it was.

But there is no point to it, this wanting.

The past is locked behind a door

I do not have the key for.

I have a growing queue of things

I know would make you laugh,

But I don't know where to put them.

I mourn like you're dead.

If you had asked me to stay,

I would not have said no.

It would never mean yes.

I used to say I'd know you anywhere,

But it's getting harder.

Time, cruel and unrelenting,

Is carving you away.

I forget the reasons,

But I loved you once,

Remember?

Was it all just an echo in the wind?

A fragile dream that shattered at dawn?

I swear, I felt you—

The way your hands memorized my skin,

The way your breath tangled with mine,

Like I was something sacred.

But now you wear silence like armor,

Eyes empty, voice cold.

You speak of me like I was a passing storm,

Never knowing I still rain inside you.

Why do you run?

Why do you carve distance between us

Only to return,

Only to rewrite the same tragedy

With different words?

I am a ruin now,

Standing where your love once lived.

Would anyone take me,

This body of broken verses,

These hands heavy with ghosts?

Oh, how I wish I could strip you of your sorrow,

But you—

You only ever dressed me in more.

I look at you, and I feel nothing.

Is this what I was waiting for?

Begging for the ache to stay,

Because pain was the last thread tying me to you.

I never wanted to heal.

Healing meant losing you twice.

Was it nothing? Or was it something

I should have held onto forever?

All that lingers is the pain—

A slow-burning fire in an abandoned home, S

wallowing me whole, day by day,

Until there is nothing left but ashes.

And yet, I remember it all too well.

To you, it was nothing.

To me,

It was everything.

I wake to an empty dawn,

The ghost of your touch lingers,

Like echoes in a hollow room.

Fingertips trace the air,

Where your hair once curled

Between them—silken memories,

Slipping like sand.

84

Where did we shatter?

Was it a quiet crack in the night,

Or did we bleed out slowly,

Never noticing the loss

Until love was just a shadow

Fading at sunrise?

Why do you want me to hate you?

To turn this love to rust,

To carve your name in bitterness,

And call it even?

After everything—

The nights we unraveled our souls,

The silent whispers,

The promises folded into my palms—

 Do they mean nothing now?

You grow bored of me,

Tired of the weight of my love,

So you sharpen your words,

Twist the knife in slow, deliberate turns,

Hoping I will flinch,

Hoping I will break.

You want me to leave, don't you?

To burn this love down myself,

To storm away so you won't

Have to be the villain.

But I don't hate you.

Not when you turn away,

Not when your touch turns cold,

Not even when you smother me

With your indifference.

Still here,

Swallowing my pride like poison,

Gulping it down,

Yet somehow, still yearning for more.

Niharika Motyani

90

How can I ever forget your touch?

It lingers like an echo in hollow halls,

Fingertips carved into my skin,

A ghost that refuses to leave.

You sit in front of me,

Eyes vacant, hands steady,

As if you've never traced the map of my wounds,

As if my name never softened on your tongue.

Niharika Motyani

You don't know me, not anymore—

Not the scars, not the traumas,

Not the nights I folded myself

Into the shape of your absence,

Aching for a love that was never mine.

And yet, I feel your gaze,

A quiet weight pressing into my bones,

Unraveling the fragile threads

I stitched together to survive you.

I shrink beneath it,

Or maybe I dissolve—

How cruel, how empty of me

To be so full of you.

Niharika Motyani

Why don't you want me like I want you?

Why does my heart burn while yours stays untouched,

Cool as the midnight air between us,

Thick with all the words we never spoke?

Why am I the only one trapped

In a love that was never ours?

A love I built alone,

Brick by brick,

While you walked away without turning back.

Niharika Motyani

Do you ever think of me?

Even for a fleeting second,

Does my name stumble into your thoughts

Like yours crashes into mine—

Relentless, unforgiving?

Why would you come see me at 4 a.m.

If it was nothing?

If I was nothing?

Did the moonlight blur the truth,

Or did you just need a place to rest

Before leaving me in the dark again?

Niharika Motyani

I keep searching for answers

In the spaces you left behind,

But all I ever find

Is silence.

Of course, your hands will learn another's shape,

Tracing her skin like a whispered vow,

Like the way I traced constellations on your palm,

Hoping you'd see the stars in me.

Of course, you'll stand beside her in the rain,

A silent promise, a sheltering touch,

The way I stood waiting for you—

Drenched, shivering, unseen.

Of course, you'll give without being asked,

Offer your time like a quiet devotion,

The way I begged in silence,

Aching for a love that never turned my way.

And the thought of it—

The thought of you giving so easily

What I bled for in vain,

It unravels me.

My heart, a glass pane,

Shattering under the weight of knowing—

You were always capable of love,

Just never for me.

How can you look at me

Like I'm just another raindrop

That never touched your skin,

Like my name is the wind—

Heard, but never held?

Niharika Motyani

Was I just a flickering streetlight

You passed beneath,

A moment of warmth

Before you stepped into the dark?

Was I someone you met

But never wanted,

A song you let play

Without ever listening?

Was I not even worth a goodbye,

Not even worth a final page

Before you closed the book

And left me unread?

Don't you miss how we'd talk until dawn,

Like two lost stars

Trying to outshine the night?

Don't you miss my silly jokes,

My laugh—

A melody that once made you smile?

Don't you miss the way I cared,

How I held you

Like a fragile piece of sky

I never wanted to drop?

Do you seriously feel nothing?

Do you seriously not miss me?

Not even a little?

Not even us?

I'd peel oranges for you,

Let the citrus burn my open wounds,

Let the scent of longing stain my hands—

If only you would take them.

I'd carve out the sun,

Hold its fire in my palms,

Watch my skin blister and crack—

If only you would ask.

I'd set the world ablaze,

Watch it smolder into nothing,

Stand in the ruin with open arms—

If only you'd run to me.

But you never asked,

Never wanted, never turned.

And here I stand, empty and burning,

Offering you the last of me—

While you walk away whole.

I let you touch my bare skin,

As if love could be learned through touch,

As if your hands might read the scars

And understand the story I never spoke.

But you skimmed over me

Like wind over water,

Never sinking deep enough to feel

The wreckage beneath.

.

I wanted you to ask,

To care,

To make space for the silence

Between my ribs,

But you only lingered long enough

To leave me empty.

Maybe I'll spend my life

Holding funerals for what never lived,

Weaving eulogies for love

That only ever echoed—

But never came back to me.

Maybe I am a collector of unfinished things,

A curator of could-have-beens,

A hoarder of echoes that never quite fade.

That is why I cannot let go of you—

Not you, perhaps,

But the hollow outline you left behind,

The phantom weight of a hand I never held.

Maybe I do not love you,

But the way your absence lingers,

The way my heart still curves around the space

Where you never belonged.

Maybe I do not love you,

But the silence between us,

The almost-words, the half-lit moments

That never found their way to dawn.

What is it?

This ache, this quiet, this never-ending sentence

With no punctuation, no closure.

I think I will never understand.

But I do love you—

Or the idea of you,

Or the version of us that only ever existed

In the poetry of my mind.

114

You are just like coffee—

Warm in my hands,

Harsh on my tongue,

Bitter in my heart.

I sip, knowing you burn,

Knowing you leave,

But craving you still.

The steam fades,

The warmth disappears,

Yet I hold the cup,

Aching for one last taste.

Maybe the universe is whispering in the wind,

Telling me you were never meant to stay.

Maybe every near encounter, every almost,

Is just fate's cruel way of keeping me away.

How can I not run into you,

When I feel you in the hush of the night?

When your presence lingers like a ghost,

Haunting me in the absence of your light?

Maybe you were just a lesson—

A fleeting storm, not the sky.

Maybe love was never ours to hold,

Just something to teach me goodbye.

But if I was meant to lose you,

Why do I still trace your name in the stars?

Why does the universe keep you close,

But never close enough for my heart?

You felt like home in a way I never knew,

A quiet comfort I never had to seek.

But love is cruel when it only lives in one heart,

When silence is the only thing that speaks.

And yet, here I stand—aching, invisible,

While you move through the world untouched.

How foolish was I to believe in something

That only ever meant this much… to me?